Bharatiya Vidya Bhavan
Private International English School, Abu dhabi

Private International English School, a part of Bharatiya Vidya Bhavan, the pioneers in providing quality education in India, is the flagship school of Bhavans Middle East since its inception in 2010 through K-12. Spearheaded by a great visionary Mr. N.K. Ramachandran Menon, along with his two children, Mr. Sooraj Ramachandran and Ms. Divya Rajesh Ramachandran as Vice Chairman and Director, with Mr. Suresh Balakrishnan as Principal at the helm, the campus offers an all-round development with special emphasis on achieving excellence through innovation, the vision we nurture with each learner who has enrolled with us. Being a progressive school, the management and leaders believe in equipping the students with 21st century skills. Apart from excelling in academics, the school has proved its mettle in myriad fields, including sports, and fine arts, and stands as a sturdy ambassador of environment protection. Indubitably, with all the documented evidence and scroll of accolades, the school is rated Very Good by ADEK consecutively for two years.

At Private International English School, we take immense pride in providing a nurturing and scaffolding learning environment, coupled with top-tier teaching quality that serves as the cornerstone of our mission. Our commitment is to inspire and motivate our students, enhancing experiential education at every step. We prioritize the development of 21st-century skills, ensuring that our students are well-prepared for the challenges and opportunities of the future. Our students have the opportunity to refine their communication, teamwork, leadership, and problem-solving skills and to transform themselves into global citizens.

English Language
Whims and Words
(An Anthology of Stories & Poems)
Compiled by:
Bharatiya Vidya Bhavan
Private International English School, Abu dhabi

Published in November 2023
by Decan Imprint Publishing Co.
Reg. Off: Sharjah Publishing City
Free Zone Sharjah, UAE.
Phone: 00971-551830334
Email : decanimprint@gmail.com

Cover Design :Ratheesh
Printed at
Manipal Technologies Ltd

14/23-24/Sl.No.14/ 400/18.6NS
ISBN 978-93-94472-67-9

Whims and words

(An Anthology of Stories & Poems)

Compiled by

Private International English School

decan imprint

Foreword

It is with overwhelming contentment that I pen my thoughts about the maiden attempt of a few of our dear students of compiling their literary works into a book. When the flagbearers of Decanimprint approached us with their igniting idea of working with schools towards publishing books, a distant dream of some of the budding writers was walking closer to them. The 15 poems and almost similar number of stories in this collection disclose the universality and diversity of thoughts our growing generation keeps abreast. It is quite promising and consoling to understand they enjoy the enchanting beauty of books. They find time to be with the world around and let their hearts dive deep into the magnificence of its infinity. They shuttle their thoughts between the real and the unreal and share the joy offered in the world of fiction but remain grounded to the reality. There are a good number of appealing and relatable characters who would help even a grown-up reader assimilate the beauty and creativity of their creators. When smaller children picked topics of fantasy, the senior secondary chose certain serious themes of like war and the unending cries it inflicts in men. Some are open enough to rip open their hearts and mourn their scattered love. Our bafflement will lead to conviction when we see them wielding certain literary devices like imagery, allegory, and symbolism with ease. Overall, with this small collection of works, our children filled my heart with hopes and confidence. There is no reason for you to have a different feeling.

Suresh Balakrishnan
Principal
Private International English School.

ACKNOWLEDGEMENT

"Whims and Words" represents the confluence of boundless imaginations and limitless creativity within a group of inquisitive children. This enchanting anthology of stories and poems found its way to the prestigious Sharjah Book Fair in 2023, thanks to the consistent support of numerous benevolent souls.

Our heartfelt gratitude is extended to our Vice Chairman, Sri Sooraj Ramachandran, for initiating discussions that paved the way for publication. We also owe a debt of thanks to our Principal, Sri Suresh Balakrishnan, whose constant guidance and mentorship played a pivotal role in bringing this project to fruition.

A special tribute goes out to the Department of English for their role in inspiring our young talents to weave their thoughts into captivating verses. Our applause extends to all the students who set free the reins of their imaginations and shared their fantastical creations.

We would like to express our appreciation to the Senior Leadership Team of PIES for their invaluable encouragement throughout the process. Mr. Ratheesh deserves a special commendation for his spot-on design work on the cover page.

Last but certainly not least, we extend our heartfelt thanks

to Mr. Ashokkumar and 'Kairali Publications' for their instrumental role in making this dream a reality.

With gratitude

Editorial Team - PIES

CONTENTS

MAGICAL CREATIONS
Ansh Kapoor 5-B

Books lead me to wonderful lands,
Above the mountains or dunes of sand.
Turning the pages gives me delight.
In my mind, books ignite a shining light.
With tales of magicians, aliens, and kings,
Books help me find amazing things.
Improving my vocabulary,
increasing my imagination,
Books are indeed magical creations!
So read, read, read my friend,
Money on books is money well spent!

SPACE
Asad 8 A

In the cosmos rare, dreams take flight,
Stars aglow, a celestial delight.
Across infinite realms, mysteries reside,
As stardust whispers, secrets confide.
Through nebulas veiled, wonders unfold,
A cosmic hold, a story untold.
Planets unseen, a celestial treasure,
Unveiling the unknown, a rare measure.
We venture beyond, where few have tread.
In the rare expanse, a realm apart,
Awe-inspiring, it captures the heart.
For in its vastness, we truly see,
The rare beauty of the cosmic decree.

THE UNEXPECTED FINDING

Avanthika Suresh 8C

CHAPTER 1
Journey through the Multiverse

It was a peaceful day for Jack and Jaime. Suddenly their doorbell rang. To their surprise, they saw their Uncle Tom who was an archeologist. They invited him to their house to have some snacks. As Uncle Tom was talking with their parents, he gave Jack and Jaime an antique clock which he had bought from an antique shop. He thought that the children would be happy to have an antique clock in their house.

After a few hours, he left their house to go to his excavation site. Then too Jack and Jaime were observing the clock and they didn't feel something was right about it.

The next day they forgot about the clock and went to school. On returning, they thought of setting the time in the clocks as they didn't have an alarm clock in their room. They rushed to their room and ran towards the clock and picked it up. Along with the clock they returned to the hall where they sat on the sofa and started to set the time.

Jamie looked at her mother's phone to get the precise time whereas Jack twisted the knob to set the time. Jamie told "It is 1:30 p.m.". And Jack set the time as 1:30 p.m. Soon it asked the date and month according to which it automatically set the day. Jaime set it to the 11th of June which was a Thursday but when they set the date it showed as Friday. They tried in different ways to make it Thursday, but it went all in vain. They were about to give up when Jack found a secret compartment at the back of the clock. He opened it to find a secret button which he pressed. As soon as they pressed it, they felt a jerk, but they thought it was a normal feeling and went out to play. To their horror, they saw everything was made from stone, even the trees! Their friends turned into moving stone statues. They were really horrified. They reckoned it was all because of the clock.

Will they find a way back home or will they get trapped? Read on to find out.

CHAPTER 2
JOURNEY THROUGH THE WORLD OF PETRAS

They were conscious of their anxiety as they noticed a few changes but were unable to make sense of what had taken place. They began looking everywhere for anything connected to the people and things that they already knew about and had used to deal with the situation. Although they were anxious, they had the courage to face the issue and tried to remain calm. They eventually concluded that they were in another UNIVERSE. They quickly discovered that they were unable to undo what they had done to the clock. They chose to go even though they were concerned that their parents would look for them. So, in order to return to the UNIVERSE, they had to act quickly. Jack and Jamie made the decision to look around to learn more about the area or to comprehend what happened in this region of the world where everyone is in horrible condition rather than living a regular life.

Soon Jack discovered a strange box in their backyard. Jamie daringly opened the box and found a piece of paper, which explained the amount of space debris to this region of the world. Its name was PETRAS, and it had formerly been a wealthy planet identical to Earth. This pitiful state has now developed as a result of the development of harmful rays from the space debris, which has not been properly handled and has reached an extreme stage.

They now realized that they were in a MULTIVERSE, which is very similar to the UNIVERSE in which we currently dwell. After realizing the significance of studying the elimination of this space debris and observing its harshest effects on this region.

CHAPTER 3
The Epilogue

They soon made the choice to return to the clock and resolve the issue so they could resume their regular lives. They made every effort to create the clock exactly how they wanted it, but in vain. Jamie and Jack were dissatisfied and worried that this region of the world would become their home. Jamie threw the clock out of frustration, and fortunately it hit on the appropriate button, allowing them to return to their regular lives. They could now hear someone yelling their names angrily as they lay in their bed. They opened their eyes to see their mother glaring at them and screaming at them to get ready for school since it was already too late. They feared looking at the clock to check the time. However, it was more like daydreaming about their trip through the antique clock that their uncle had given them.

They were also taken aback when their teacher Ms. Susan explained the launching of rockets and satellites into space, how critical is every launch which might be either successful or failure and the amount of space junk that gets accumulated in space.

Ms. Susan then called a student in the classroom and asked the following question: Do you understand the impact and situation we will encounter when we get such space debris from another universe?

Jack and Jamie stared at each other in agitation.

THE BEST DAY YET
Avantika 7D

Once there was a girl named Emma. Emma was a kind, carefree, and simple girl. She appreciated everything she had received in life, but there was one longing that never left her heart – the desire to be friends with Diana. But there was one problem. She was too shy to talk to her and kept doubting herself and making assumptions that Diana didn't like her .

The reasons for her shyness in approaching Diana were that Diana had numerous popular friends, she held the title of the most popular student at Kendrick High, and Diana was highly extroverted, while Emma was distinctly introverted.

Then, at night after supper Emma decided to tell her dear diary about Diana. She told her diary how much she wanted to be friends with her and went to sleep.

The next morning, Emma rushed to eat her breakfast since she was late. Thankfully, the bus waited for her. She sat down in the bus relieved about it. After an hour she reached school. The first period was Maths and guess what, it was a surprise test! Emma got stuck on this trigonometry question. Fortunately, when the test scores came, she got it right.

The first few periods went on sluggishly. Finally, it was lunch break. Emma ate her peanut butter sandwich with joy as she was famished. It was science period after lunch, her favorite period. As she heard Ms. Appleberry's lecture she peered to the side and saw

Diana and her friends wearing expensive rose gold dresses and fancy bracelets. Emma watched in awe and wished she could be that popular in school.

Finally, it was dispersal. Emma got on her bus and started thinking of talking to Diana about being friends with her but alas, what could she do! She was not as talented as Dians was, and could never talk to such a large group of people.

That night, as Emma gazed out of her bedroom window, she spotted a shooting star and made a fervent wish for Diana to become her friend. In her dream there was something blurry blue and foggy. The experience was so mystical that it felt like she had entered a truly bizarre world.

"Who are you?" shouted Emma.

"It's me genie, "said the genie.

"Aren't you supposed to exist in Aladdin's magic lamp?" asked Emma curiously.

The genie laughed and said "I am your creation. Didn't you know whatever you wish for comes true. You just need to tell me your wish.

"Are you joking?" said Emma.

"No, not at all just tell me your wish dear?"

"Ok, I want to be friends with a girl called Diana, but I'm too shy?"

"Why don't you talk to her?" asked genie.

"I have tried to, but I am just too shy." said Emma.

"Your wish is my command", so saying, the genie snapped his finger and disappeared.

"Emma, Emma!",

Emma's eyes became bigger than her stomach. She was late to school and slept through two periods.

She rushed to school and arrived at the 3rd period in Mr. Stinklefieston's class. Mr Stinklefieston was a very bossy teacher and demanded everyone to finish their work in a day's time. Else, they will have to face the consequences.

Mr. Stinklefieston had a long narrow mustache, square glasses which were bigger than his eyes, and a fiery face which turned red every second. Once Mr. Stinklefieston was so angry at a student that he was made to stand at the back of the class and complete the whole semester's work since he took a day off from school. So, when Emma went to Mr. Stinklefieston's class, he appeared to be redder than the tomatoes and told her to complete the complete notes of the biology chapter.

After a few more periods it was recess, she thought during recess Diana would talk to her but there was no luck. She thought that it was pointless to talk to Diana. She took spaghetti from the canteen and twirled it around feeling useless. Finally, school was over for the day and Emma went back home sitting at the corner of her bed and started crying as the night became darker and darker.

"Emma, Emma! Wake up! It's me, your fairy godmother "

"Yesterday I saw Genie and today it's you!" said Emma, irritated.

"Fine, I'm still your dream but if you really want to be friends with Diana you must finish the game "

"What game?" asked Emma.

"There are three rounds in the game. If you complete all the rounds, you will be able to be friends with Emma. The game will help you to improve your patience, loyalty, and generosity. Friendship things you know!" said the Fairy Godmother.

"I'm in", said Emma desperately.

"Then shall the game begin." said the fairy godmother, ready than ever.

The rules of the game are fairly simple: You will be given a new character in every round and you get 3 lifelines . If you finish 'em all up, you go back to the real world and can never return. So, use your lifelines wisely and there is no room for mistakes.

"Ready, set, go!"

The first round is chess. This game requires absolute patience to get the hang of it.

Emma was competing with an AI. So, now you know how difficult it is.

First Emma moved a pawn, and the game continued. In a little while….. "Oh no checkmate!" One of her lifelines was already used up. This time Emma thought of fooling the AI and pretended as if she was about to take the knight but took the queen instead and she won. Emma was so happy that she won the first round. Only two more to go…

In the second round, Emma changed into a new character. She was a princess who had the most beautiful hair in the town. To go to the next round, she needed to cross the sea but there was a sea serpent weeping and blocking her way.

"Why are you crying?" asked Emma.

"My beautiful moustache has been cut. Now everyone thinks I am hideous", said the sea serpent sobbing.

Emma without thinking cut off her beautiful hair and gave it to the serpent. Now she could go to the last round.

In the last round, Emma needed to practise honesty. She went back in time and saw the time when she stole some money from her friend. She went and talked to her past self about it.

Now Emma completed all the three rounds, and this excited her as she could befriend Diana!

"Ring, Ring"

"Aaaaah!" shouted Emma.

"What happened?" said Emma's mother in a worried tone. She just broke her favourite vase.

"Oh, nothing, nothing", said Emma relaxing herself.

"You just broke my favourite vase!" said Emma's mother.

"I'm sorry!" said Emma.

"I forgive you but don't repeat it. Now off to school Emma!" said her mother.

Emma ate her salad and bread and reached her school bus. She revised her test chapters and was ready for Biology class.

The first few periods flew fast and then after a while to her utter surprise, Diana called her for lunch. They sat together and talked together. It was as if they had been friends all along.

She then went back home and wrote in her diary that this was her "best day yet". Then she got a message. It was Diana. She had Emma's number. She asked if she wanted to meet her today at her mother's house. Emma screeched with excitement and went to her house and had a fantastic evening with all her friends.

THE SUNLIT SKY
Ayisha Sunil 7A

I stared silently at the sunlit sky
That shone over the feathered fly.
I gazed at the frozen mountain peak
Towering over the valley, harsh and bleak.
I looked down at the river's grace
Where colourful fish lay without brace.
I sighed and leaned on my chair
And went on with my lazy stare.

DÍA DE MUERTOS
Ayush Satheesh 8A

It is the time to honour those
who have shed their mortal coil,
And to adorn those masks in accordance
with our Hoyle,
To drape the walls of our departed ones,
In our ofrendas,
where they are immortalized by our young.

All around, bright shades of purples and oranges,
With bursts of pink,
that embrace our phalanges.
Festoons of our marigold,
Towers of calaveras that grace our altars fourfold.

Bringing delicacies and night-caps during the ballad,
That were once partial to their palate.
Setting them upon the ofrenda,
Pondering, the epoch
when we will reunite with our abuela.

THE BATTLE THAT NEVER RECEDES
Deva Nanda Manoj 12 A

Darkness has surmounted the throne of my heart,
There's a commotion in my mind,
The riots seem eternal,
The riot between the positive and negative
No sign of it abating,
Ah!
A brutal massacre has taken place,
In my mind,
Every tiny tinge of optimism has been assassinated,
My hands are bathed in red,
For my heart bleeds,
It bleeds out the last tinge of optimism I had in me,
The last burning candle of optimism has been extinguished by
the brutal wind of negativity,
My heart feels hollow,
But my feelings are deep,
I am clinging to the last branch of hope,
Although I can hear it creak,
But.......I know I will never fall,
For I can feel the two hands,
Holding me upright,

Those two hands, which weigh heavier than my soul and heart together,
The entire world might shoot arrows of distrust at me,
The entire world might throw stones of hatred at me,
But these two souls will protect me with the shield of eternal love,
'Cause I am their heart,
I am their soul,
Every heartbeat of theirs belongs to me,
And mine to them,
For they make me,
The world hears me through words of mouth,
But they hear the voice of my heart, my mind, my soul,
Even better than myself,
The dense jungle of life,
Is hilariously dangerously odd ,
Sometimes,
I might be able to sit on the lap of mother nature
and lose myself in its aesthetic beauty,
At other times,
I might have to encounter the wildest of beasts,
But fear holds no space in my heart,
For my heart has no void,
Every tiny void…. is occupied by those two souls,
For their love reigns in my heart,
And nothing can defeat that to the throne of my heart,
I might get washed by the sea,
But, I'll never drown,
For they have never told me to never burn in the fire of life,
But they have taught me to rise from the remnant ashes of life,
And that makes my life,
That makes me!

THE WORLD IN A BOTTLE OF INK
Dhruv Anand 12B

She sits at her desk and twirls her pen.

The mist that hangs over the traffic lights, Will be waved away by a gentle hand.

Commuters in a sea of fog

Will see clearly. Planes will land Safely. A look heavenward, Now impossible, will reveal, And over white wine and veal,

Silken ties will not be able to conceal, Blood spilled, that the bleeding did not see, By smiling faces against an unsaid plea.

She twirls her pen.

A sudden indiscriminate electric shock, Administered through spiral-bound copies, And online downloads.

Torn pages making inroads,

Words in a corner of the entertainment section. The man buying groceries will not be safe,

Nor the orator that sits in the café,

Nor the driver of the yellow Rolls-Royce, Whose skin the camel-hair wool does chafe. The boy whistling away on a stack of hay, Will not be safe.

She twirls her pen.

The one will become the many, and life will start to spill, Into the squares and the halls,

Into the fervor of bars and the streetwalker's calls.

The gallop of feet on pavement and the crackle of rage, Will make the world a stage and the acts footsteps.

The shedders of blood will repent with every printed page. The minister's windshield wipers that do not work,

Will admit amidst the rain presences that now only lurk.

A slouching human race will stand up straight, For she, twirling her pen, like the first time, Retains the edge the foamy waves of experience Could not wash away.

She twirls her pen, and the world comes to a standstill.

THE ROAD TAKEN
Dhruva Patadiya 12 A

Oh to go down the road not taken
but i'm not as brave
so down i go, the road that always was
i fade against the background
and the realization hits, that i'm nobody special
but at least it's easier to hide in here
here, where my troubles are nothing but mere complaints
here, where shadows like me
have glistened their way to the top
maybe we're all just shadows too afraid to fade further
and so, i run,
but only to reach where the two roads diverge
and maybe sometimes
the further you fade, the more vivid you return
so i chose the road always taken
and that has made all the difference.

A WALK IN HEAVEN AND HELL
Hajra Fatima 9B

Here in Hell, and there I see
Burned trees and seas of misery,
Here and there the Hellhound stares
Waiting for the water to turn
Bloody red.

Here in Heaven, Yes it's true
Angels fly and there is a truce
And don't worry I won't lie
That when you die you can fly.
So, do good deeds and avoid Hell.

Hey! Wait for me! I'll be there soon, wait and see.

THOSE DAYS
Hiya Brahmbhatt 6 A

Those days I would just sit and play .
I would think it was the best way to say
"Hooray!" in another way.
I loved to stare at those trees which swayed.
Every day was an interesting day.
Even today days are interesting but not just
like those days.
But still I have the keys to that fun way,
I will enjoy every day, what do you say?

A GENTLE PUSH FROM A TRUE FRIEND IS ALL WE NEED
Hridya Girish Nair 6E

Once upon a time, there lived two childhood friends Gopi and Gitish. Both worked in a car garage. Gopi was a mechanic and was good at his work but was a bit too casual in his life while Gitish was a painter in the same Garage and was more ambitious than Gopi. They lived in a small hut with their wives and two children. Their lives were tough.

One day Gitish's mother suddenly fell ill. He with his family had to shift to their hometown where his mother lived. Knowing that he won't be coming back soon, Gitish gave away all his mere savings to help Gopi. "What stupidity are you doing by giving away your life savings to your friend", remarked his wife. "Gopi is like my brother. He is very talented and will reach great heights in life," said Gitish. He will definitely help us back when required.

Days and weeks passed by. There was no return of Gitish. Gopi went to Gitish's hometown and found nobody there, he inquired but could not find Gitish and his family. Gopi was dejected, lonely and helpless. With no other way, he started to focus on his passion. Using his friend's savings, he decided to design a new car engine and started working day and night. His hard work finally found result as he invented one of the best car engines.

Gradually, his engines were in great demand. He started a car company. He became rich and famous. Even after all this success, he was sad and his search for his best friend continued. One day he visited a village in search of a land for building his new factory. He saw a few children playing football match on that land. Gopi said, "Children you are at the best time of your life". Even I had a good childhood and had a very good friend. Like you, we used to play together. We grew up together and worked in a small garage. One day he left me to take care of his mother and never came back. Now I am successful, but my best friend is not with me. As Gopi further described about Gitish, he suddenly noticed a girl weeping. He asked, why are you crying. The girl replied that the story you told is about my father.

Gopi was overwhelmed and was eager to meet Gitish. She took Gopi to their home. The good old friends were quite happy to meet each other after long years!

Gopi asked Gitish, "Why didn't you come back to meet me all these years?

Gitish said, "I am so happy with your achievement". I knew your potential and wanted you to grow but with my presence you were too casual in life. Sometimes friends should part ways for their own good and wellbeing. Hearing all this Gopi said, you are right, when you left, I started thinking of my passion. I realized that talent is not enough, sometimes we really need a push from a good friend like you.

All my success is because of you. Gitish and his family went with Gopi and they lived together happily ever after.

LIFE
Hrishikesh 8 A

Life is a carriage
Driven by a Horse
If you whip it hard,
It will surely toss
It will turn upside down
to make you frown
So don't whip it hard
and keep kindness by your heart.

THE SHADOW
Ira Verma 5B
A Story of Mystery and Laughter.
This Story Will Surely Get the Giggles Out of You!

It was a cold and windy night. My sister and I were tucked in our bed right next to each other when suddenly I heard a noise. It was coming from my parent's bedroom. I slowly tip-toed into their room. When I opened the door, everyone had hit the sack but the window was open. When I looked out of the window and saw a shadow in our backyard, I ran downstairs to see who was there. I was exhausted after all that running. On the other hand, the shadow was gone in the snap of a finger. I looked everywhere but, they were nowhere to be found. I thought it was a dream and fell asleep on the sofa. Suddenly I was woken up by a violent shake, it was my sister. She was screaming at me, "WAKE UP, WAKE UP! It's time for school already! Take a shower and get ready, QUICKLY!" I woke up hastily and got dressed. The bus was about to leave when I got on just in time.

My Buddies of School

Then I sat right next to my buddies, Aashi, and Saraswati. We then gossiped about my weird 'dream' for a while, laughed, and had fun. In the end, Aashi then asked me, "Hey Ira, when's your birthday party? Your birthday is just 4 days away!". I thought for a while and answered, "Well… I'm not that sure. My parents haven't decided but, when they do, I'll let you guys know!" Right when I said these words,

we were on our school's playground. We got down and parted ways to our classrooms. The first period was Mathematics. While ma'am was talking, I saw the shadow again. I then decided to sneak out of the class and follow it but, gave up. Otherwise, I would miss a lot of notes in just one period.

A few days passed and I was still traumatized by it. Then I got the guts to follow it. Just before I could go, I told my friends to write my notes for me since I would miss the class. The shadow kept on moving and moving…. It had been 20 minutes and I was giving up hope of finding anything.

The Plot Twist

I then suddenly saw a box. I ran inside and saw a long hallway. In the end, there was an enormous door. I looked around just to make sure no one was spying on me and I barged in. On my first step, everyone screamed with joy, "HAPPY BIRTHDAYYY!! MAY GOD BLESS YOUUU!!"

I was perplexed. I completely forgot that it was even my birthday! Everyone I knew was there. I had a pile of gifts waiting for me. It turned out that my dad had won the lottery and he did this to make me feel merry (which he did). And that shadow was really my sister! I then took deep breaths and calmed myself down. After a while, I went closer to the heart of the box-like room. I at a distance saw a small, cozy little table with a huge 6-tier cake on top! It said, 'Happy Birthday Ira' and my age '10'. There were almost 25 candles on the cake! In the end, my mother gave me a dress and told me to wear it. It was red in colour and after I wore it, I looked gorgeous and absolutely stunning! We all then took a break and had lots of food and drinks. First and foremost, we all decided to play games. The first game was the classic musical chairs. Then we played hide n seek, followed by freeze tag.

More Surprises!

In the end, all the school buses came to drop off all the students. I then did what I was craving for. OPENING THE GIFTS! I then got all my favourites like Lego sets, Colouring books, new stationery, and much more. This was the best day of my life!!! I thanked my parents for being so awesome and got a new surprise ahead of me. WE WERE GOING TO THE THEME PARKS AND WATER PARKS AND ROAMED AROUND THE WORLD!!! That means we were traveling the world! Oh, how I love my family! For the next 2 months, I didn't go to school and travelled the world with tickets to theme parks and water parks. I wish that moment could last forever!

Well, if I told you EVERYTHING the list would just never end! So, see you soon in my next book!

Good Byeeeeeeee!!!

NEW WORDS
1. Hit the sack- (IDIOM) Go to bed
2. Snap of a finger- (IDIOM) Something to happen quickly
3. Violent- (ADJECTIVE) To hit, hurt, or damage something or someone
4. Hastily- (ADVERB) To do something quickly
5. Gossiped-(VERB) To talk
6. Traumatized- (VERB) To be left shocked by something or someone
7. Perplexed-(ADJECTIVE) Confused or puzzled
8. Merry- (ADJECTIVE) Happy or joyful
9. First and foremost-(PHRASE) Most importantly

"MR. PHOENIX NASTY- A FOOTBALL ROLE MODEL ONE COULD EVER ASK FOR."

Krithin Tanga 4B

Once upon a time, there lived the best football player in the world and this story belongs to him. Phoenix Nasty was born during the winter season into a middle-class family in Great Britain. He used to live with his grandparents, parents, and five siblings in a small cottage. As Mr. Nasty was the eldest among his siblings, he also used to nurture his siblings. One day, to make his youngest sibling happy through play, Mr. Nasty showcased his skills in playing a ball with his foot. Soon Mr. Nasty saw a surprising response from his youngest sibling. This made Mr. Nasty exhibit more of his skills with football, like passing the ball to other siblings and shooting the ball by kicking it higher towards the goal. His youngest sibling was amazed by Mr. Nasty's playing skills with a ball and screamed to him, "You are the best brother and a player one could ever ask for". This response from Mr. Nasty's brother made Mr. Nasty dream of having a career in football sport. Coming from an educational and middle-class family background, Mr. Nasty's parents never agreed to his decision to become a professional football player.

A few months later in his school, the International Football Sports Meet was announced, and Mr. Nasty was interested in participating in it. He asked his parents about the participation, and they had a deal with him. If Mr. Nasty wins the game and gets a scholarship from this specific event, he can choose his career as a football player and if he loses, then he needs to concentrate on his education. Mr. Nasty took this as a golden opportunity to prove his football skills not only to his parents but to the whole world. He accepted the challenge and worked hard towards achieving it with determination, consistency, and passion. In this process of practising football, Mr. Nasty became more focused, attentive, patient, and more resilient. His communication skills became better, and he became more self-confident than ever.

Mr. Nasty's parents noticed better grades, overall academic and social functioning during this phase of Mr. Nasty's life. This made Mr. Nasty's parents realise how determined their son was in pursuing his dream of becoming a football player. And as everyone expected, Mr. Nasty won the international football sports meet along with his teammates and was awarded the best player of the match. Mr. Nasty's parents were not only happy with his achievement but were proud to see their son shine in many ways and become a better person. A few years later, Mr. Phoenix Nasty represented Great Britain and played for the nation. He became a role model for many all over the world.

Moral of the story- Mr. Nasty's story helps us to understand that "By performing righteously one's duty with hard work, consistency, and determination one can achieve one's dream. Also, it will help the person to become a better functioning individual."

SCHOOL LIFE
Mahi Bhatia 11 E

These years are the ones we will never get back,

We learn, we experience and to be someone we build a track.

We sow the seed for the tree of knowledge, we build the foundation to the city of life,

This is just the beginning of the experience of the nostalgic "school life".

From little children to young adults we grow,

We learn how to engage in friendships, and we learn how relationships can break.

When it goes from "I don't want to go" to "I don't want it to end" we don't realise,

Some days just 40 minutes is too long yet some days even seven hours don't suffice.

We have spent so much time here yet there's so much more,

Now it's time to break out and be your own person, it's time to open that door.

It's time to walk the set track with the knowledge, understanding, experience and discipline gained along the way,

This may be the end of the marvellous school life but there's so much more to learn and so much more to say.

LAVENDER LOVE
Minha Haris 11 A

"Don't worry" I told my roommate as I coughed up more flowers all over the floor, but his face showed only that. The flowers I spewed are covered with blood; their soft petals drooping, but beautiful all the same. I bend down to pick them up but Callum puts his hand on my shoulder and pulls me up.

"You get some sleep, I'll clean up," he says, tears threatening to fall from his eyes.

I nod and move towards the washroom to clean up. I look back just as I was about to open the door to find Callum picking up the flowers and taking a few seconds to observe them before throwing them in the trash. I enter the washroom and look in the mirror and see myself, my lips glistening with blood and small lavender petals stuck to my face.

I wash them off and head back. I lay on my bed and during this stillness I feel the roots curl tighter around my lungs. Bittersweet thing it is; Hanahaki. A disease caused by unrequited love. Of course, there are ways to solve it, either get the person to love you back or get a surgery, at the cost of forgetting you ever loved them. If you don't do anything, you die.

Days go by and the effects have only been getting worse. It's been weeks since I've experienced normality, it's not just me either. Callum's been getting more insistent, I know he can't bear to see me like this, but I can't bear to do the surgery either. The thought has crossed my mind a lot but in the end, I always shake it off. I've always been one to hate being left out. Couldn't help but feel like the surgery would leave me out of my own life.

I don't go to classes anymore; my body has been weakened far beyond my control. Yet, I avoid the solution. Is death better than losing love?

I wake up in the middle of the night, gasping for air. My throat has been scratched raw; breaths raspy. I'm drowning in my own blood. I clench my fists and head to the bathroom coughing violently. More petals fall as I bend my head over the sink. Still beautiful. I remember a quote from a book I read not too long ago, "Beauty is terror, Whatever we call beautiful, we quiver before it". Never been more true.

I wash up and stare in the mirror. I'm watching from afar, viewing my own body from the outside. Everything feels so fulfilling yet empty. Why did I decide this is how I go out? Why do I not fight back? Why lavenders? The last question sticks for a while, but I'm too tired to search for answers. I go back to sleep.

Another week passes. I'm back home now. I don't leave my room. It's almost time. I can feel it. I imagine my insides, swirled with roots and lavender petals. I lie in my bed and stare at the ceiling. My thoughts are my only company. I think about life. And death. Whichever is closer.

I think of my family, my friends, how would they react when they found out? Surely they'd cry, surely they saw it coming too. I think about her. The reason I'm here. My room starts to spin as I feel my heart clench. I feel the roots make their way, tightening, coursing, writhing. I close my mouth and constrict my throat to stop the petals. My vision blurs. My thoughts settle. It is eerily quiet. A bittersweet thing it is; Love. I close my eyes. I go to sleep. I don't wake up.

THE ENCHANTED EYE VIEW
Minha Haris 11A

The sound of Hiraki's footsteps were lost among the crowd as she desperately made her way through it. It was unlike her to be in a rush, but that morning she went to pick up her glasses from repair, only to be held up by the pharmacist there. 'The perfect pair make everything look better', she kept insisting. Now she found herself clutching onto her messenger bag as she weaved through the dozens. It was only when she reached the familiar bylane that she escaped the crowd.

She continued to power walk her way across the sidewalk, pulling her coat tighter around her. The Vernal Equinox holiday in Japan was only a few days away, yet the cold winter breeze didn't cease. Hiraki stole a quick glance at her watch, 7:52. She looked back up and was met by the sight of an antique gift shop. 'The Lucky Cat' the sign read. She passed by the store everyday but something was different, or so she felt. Slowly her feet deviated from their trained route and began making its way to the worn out wooden door.

Hiraki gently pushed it open. The soft chimes of the bell by the entrance filled the little store.

"Coming throughhhh!" yelled a little boy as he ran through the aisle and almost right into her

"Yuki" Called out an elderly woman behind the counter "Don't scare the customers!"

"Sorry Sobo!"

Hiraki matches the smile on the woman's face, while she tries to decide what to do next. The incessant pull that she felt till now had disappeared. It would be rude to just leave, she thinks to herself. It'd be better to take a look around at least. She began walking down one of the aisles, pretending to be interested in all the different trinkets they had to offer. Meanwhile her mind was elsewhere, trying to figure out the best way to leave unnoticed. She had to get to her office soon.

"HI"

Hiraki's eyes widened, and her hand went to her heart as she turned around, "Hello"

"I'm Yuki" The boy introduced himself with a wide smile, toy trains clutched in his hand.

"And I'm Hiraki, nice to meet you Yuki". She turns back only for her thoughts to be interrupted again.

"What do you want to buy?" He asked eagerly.

"I'm not sure", she took a glance at the display once more. "What would you suggest?"

"Hmmm……How about this?" He picked up a kokeshi doll.

"No..I have plenty of those already" She shook her head.

"This?"

"Oh, a Daruma…My friend got me one last week, sorry"

"This?"

"No"

"This?"

"Something more practical?"

Yuki took one last hard look around the whole aisle and his eyes visibly brightened as they landed on something at the far end. He went down, picked the object up and proudly held it up for Hiraki to see.

"It's a keychain! For your bag"

"I'm not sure Yuki, it's not really my style" She took it into her hands, it was a small figure of a lucky cat. She held it against her bag, the bright colours of the cat in stark contrast with the neutral browns and greens she often wore.

"It doesn't have to be."

"What do you mean?"

"It doesn't have to be *your* style for you to enjoy it. It's small and pretty, the pink paws remind me of the cherry blossoms outside." He said pointing.

"Oh…."

Hiraki had been doing things without wasting a second for as long as she could remember. What was the point if she wasn't being productive, she had forced herself to believe. It was almost spring despite the cold air; the full bloom cherry blossom trees were a clear indication of it. She hadn't even noticed them……..

"So?" Yuki questioned

Hiraki's mind was made in that moment.

"*I don't knooowww*" She teased with a playful smile.

"Ughhh" Yuki rolled his eyes and went to pick up his trains again which he had abandoned at some point. "Fine you choose something then."

"I'll try" She watched as he disappeared into the store rooms.

She let out a quiet chuckle and made her way to the counter "I'll take this." She placed down the keychain and gave the woman a bright smile.

As she stepped out of the store, the bell chimed once more. Hiraki stood on the sidewalk and took a deep breath. She took in the sight. The cherry blossoms really were perfect. She checked her watch again, 7:58. Office hours would begin soon and Hiraki resumed her journey there. But this time, she let her eyes and thoughts wander. It was a beautiful day. She thought back to the early morning and smiled to herself, *the perfect pair might make everything look better* but the perfect view makes the best of everything. The Enchanted Eye View.

PLEASE DON'T LEAVE
Nidhi Dileep 11C

As her departure became certain
It left a stain
On my mind. As she leaves,
I see the fallen leaves
She said people you love will always be a star,
But now I feel like we're miles afar.
I have fallen into a pit,
Full of darkness
Along with my feelings, the pit becomes wider
And deeper.

How is it possible,
That I thought her departure was impossible?
I try to conceal
The pain, but it is real.

THE STARSHIP JOURNEY
Rehan Chandra 8C

I was comfortably resting at home on my cozy armchair, staring at the news on my TV. Suddenly, a headline popped up: "Win a ride to another galaxy on a STARSHIP! Book your tickets now and win the prize".

I was startled. How could they create a starship that could travel to another galaxy? And now it is on for a RAFFLE ticket. Anyways, they DID make it, so I, as usual, needed to book my ticket FAST. I was practically SPRINTING to my laptop. After booking, I prayed to get the golden ticket. But I had never won a lottery before, so I thought this ticket is going to be of no use to me. The following day, I woke up in the morning, made myself a coffee, read a newspaper, and checked my mailbox as I did every day regularly. But when I opened it, I was FLABBERGASTED! There was a golden ticket, telling "You have won the chance to enter and ride the grand Starship, with your team!" The crew members' names were also listed below.

To make sure that it was not FRAUD, I double-checked by calling another team. Thankfully, they did not get the ticket. I called my team members and we met each other in a camper, which was the only vehicle fitting all of us comfortably, as it was a long journey.

We reached the FlyBird Square. The environment of the launch site was barren. Of course, we did not expect it to be green and populated as it gets really hot when the spacecraft lifts off and there would be too much SMOKE. We finally reached the launch pad, where they displayed to us the MAGNIFICENT starship that we were boarding. They directed us to the entrance through an elevator. I say the name of the craft, "SpaceShark I". It truly DID look like a shark with wings. We boarded and took our seats. It was made of leather and lined with blue velvet. The starship took off, leaving behind a trail of stardust.

The journey went smooth and easy, and we were soon out of the earth's atmosphere, the Solar System, and finally the Oort cloud. We were soon out of the Milky Way and reached an undiscovered galaxy. We found a Maple leaf-shaped planet and found a perfect spaceport to land in, but we ran out of fuel just as we reached the planet's atmosphere. So, we crash-landed upon its surface.

The engine shut down just in time as it landed, so there was no further accident. We struggled out of the ship and soon found out that no one was hurt. We set out on an adventure half an hour later, after we had snacks. We stayed close together to make sure we didn't get lost. I heard some rustling sounds and became alert as to find the SLIGHTEST movements other than the team and myself. I came to find a shadow near me. I informed the others and stood still, not moving a bit. Then another shadow appeared. Then the third. Just thinking it was the alien I saw in a horror movie last week made my teeth quiver. But, when the other-worldly creatures came closer, we discovered that they were tiny, cute creatures. Still, I maintained a safe distance and stayed alert if it CHANGED its TONE, but it never did. Those heartwarming inhabitants of this strange planet were really kind. They provided us with shelter and food, which was really strange as I had never eaten that kind of a dish before. I was just relieved I wasn't EXTINCT!

Meanwhile, they assisted us to repair our ship, which was a total mess. The core was damaged (the core is basically the ENGINE of the starship). But we still did not run out of luck as the rare substance on earth, is an abundant and common resource on the planet we arrived on. After rebuilding our starship, we thanked the aliens for their help and presented them with a banquet of English breakfast. They were happy to try the food they had never eaten before and found it super-tasty. As we left for our home planet, earth, I shed a tear. I was sad to leave those helpful new creatures but was equally eager to see my species and my own family again. When we reached earth, we wanted to protect the aliens, so we lied about the aliens that they were angry, ferocious beasts who were about to devour us and that we escaped in the nick of time.

And then, friends, our adventure ended with us in one single piece, but don't worry. We will visit our little friends again and keep presenting them with gifts, and we'll find interesting new elements for mankind to develop and maintain a peaceful life for the rest centuries.

OLIVER'S JOURNEY
Rima Ravichandran 11D

Once upon a time in the quaint village of Nookshire, there lived a young boy named Oliver. His heart swelled with dreams of adventure and a longing to leave the safety of his home behind. His father, Joseph, a stern but loving man, understood the restlessness of youth and decided to guide Oliver in his journey.

"Son," Joseph said, his voice brimming with wisdom, "the world beyond our village is vast and teeming with wonders. I want you to find your own path, but remember, family is the compass that will guide you back."

Wide eyed and eager, Oliver packed his bag, bidding farewell to his family. His mother, Elizabeth, embraced him tightly, whispering, "We'll be counting the days until you return."

Oliver ventured into the untamed wilderness, crossing treacherous mountains, cascading rivers, and mysterious forests. Along the way, he met a group of warriors who became his loyal companions.

One night, around a campfire, Oliver poured his heart out to his new friends, "I miss my family. I want to be brave, but sometimes I'm scared of what's ahead."

His companions exchanged knowing glances before Boris, the burly axe-wielder, spoke, "Oliver, lad, fear is but a spark that ignites our determination. Trust in yourself, and you'll overcome anything."

Determined and fortified by his friends' words, Oliver continued his journey. Finally, he stood at the edge of a precipice, gazing at a vast ocean stretched out before him. With a newfound strength in his heart, Oliver declared to the wind, "I am ready!" And he dived headfirst into the great unknown.

In the years that followed, Oliver traversed continents, battled mythical beasts, and even saved kingdoms. Yet, his thoughts always returned to the family he left behind.

One fateful day, as the setting sun painted the horizon in shades of gold, Oliver found himself standing at the village gates of Nookshire. Tears welled in his eyes as he pushed open the familiar door of his childhood home.

"Oliver!" cried his mother, her joyous laughter filling the room. Oliver's father stood beside her, tears streaming down his weathered face.

In that moment, Oliver knew that his journey had come full circle. He had found adventure, discovered his place in the world, but above all, he returned to the loving embrace of his family.

WARRIOR OF THE BATTLE

Rima Ravichandran 11D

In days of yore, when battles raged and kings did reign,
There lived a warrior, bold and brave,
with heart of steel and chain.
His armour shone like gold in sunlight,
his sword did gleam and glow,
His courage in the heat of battle,
none could ever know.
His foes did tremble at his sight,
his roar did make them flee,
For he was fierce and fearless,
a true hero of his time, you see.
He fought for what was right,
for justice and for love,
His honour untarnished,
his spirit pure from above.
In fields of battle, he did stride,
his sword held high and true,
His shield did protect him,
as he fought for what he knew.
His heart did beat with valour,
his spirit did soar,
For he was a warrior, a hero,
forevermore.

EMOTIONS
Santhosh Mahendran 9D

When we feel like a sunken boat,
When we feel a lump in our throat,
And when we can no longer hide our emotions,
And there starts the overflowing of tears blurring our vision,
Tears are liquefied emotions falling out of our eyes,
Like pearls gleamingly falling out of an oyster
hidden deep beneath the sea,
When we feel like a boat gliding smoothly across the sea,
When our lives feel merry and glee,
And when we let our happiness take over,
Now nothing can ruin our day and turn it somber,
And if happiness is plentiful and can no longer be held inside,
And there starts the overflowing of tears blurring our eyes,
Tears are liquefied emotions falling out of our eyes,
Like pearls gleamingly falling out of an oyster
hidden deep beneath the sea,
But as the saying goes, "Nothing can last forever.",
So don't say never,
Because our lives are like the tides,
They rise and fall,
And rise again.

"STRAWBERRIES"
Sarah Fatima 10E

Today, Julia and I are going to her late father's favorite place,
The strawberry fields.

His last wish was to be buried there, so whenever we visited, we
remember him, not in sadness but as a happy memory.

Julia left my hand and ran to her father's grave, placing the flowers
she had picked on the way.

"Don't worry dad! I'll get you your favorite fruits today, wild
strawberries!"

I listened to her before walking over to the huge cherry tree that
loomed over us, in the middle of the field.

Being a poet, poems keep me calm, concentrated and in control.
But after the death of my late husband, all I could write about was
him.

I started to write in my journal-

"I was the leaves and blooming flower,
While you were my supporting stem,
I took care of us,
While you gave us strength.
Soon the clouds,
Rained down,
I withered,
You drowned..."

I was about to write more but…my heart stopped me.

Right at that moment I heard Julia scream!

I dropped my pen and journal and rushed towards her, seeing her stuck in a bushel of thorns. "What's happened?" I asked,

"I was getting wild strawberries for daddy!"

I sighed, "Darling, you know the bushes are prickly, and besides we could have just bought some,"

"Yes but daddy loved fresh berries not store bought, and you're always way too sad to help me pluck some anyways…,"

"Oh…" I stopped for a second to look at her then freed her from the bush whilst we spoke.

She picked up the fallen berries and put them in her basket.

I looked at her.

Her eyes were puffy, but unlike mine, she had been crying due to being hurt from the thorns,

I had been hurt too, but…emotionally and it had taken a toll on our relationship.

My husband was buried here, so when we visit we'd be happy…

Together.

"Wait…,"

Julia turned,

"I-" I let out a deep breath I didn't know I was holding, "where can we find those strawberries?"

Her eyes turned wide, "Really?"

I nodded, and she wrapped her arms around me in a huge hug!

She looked so happy!

She grabbed my sleeve and dragged me across.

We spent the rest of the afternoon collecting and eating strawberries.

Before leaving though, I told Julia,

"We can't keep the strawberries there dear, they may get rotten,"

She looked disheartened as she was about to place the basket on the grave, "But-"

I gave her a soft smile,

"I have a better idea…"

***

> *"I was the leaves*
> *And she was our blooming flower,*
> *While you were our supporting stem,*
> *I took care of us,*
> *While you gave us strength.*
> *Soon the clouds,*
> *Rained down,*
> *I withered,*
> *You drowned,*
> *But from the flood,*
> *Of sorrow and weary,*
> *Blossomed another set,*
> *Of sweet scented strawberries."*

I laid the poem, a torn piece of paper, on his grave.
I held Julia's hand, "ready?"
She nodded,
And we both happily started towards home,
With the scent of fresh sweet strawberries filling the air.

THE MOUSE CITY
Sivakami Perumal 6B

There was a small world called mouse world where millions of mice lived. There lived two little mice named Jenny and Jerry who were best friends. They played, ate, and spent time together. But one day there was danger in the land so, the mice had to leave from the land because there were tons of cats wandering in the land to eat the mice. All the mice left expect Jenny and Jerry. Because they didn't know how to escape because they were just kids.

Then, Jenny was caught by a big black cat who was hungry. Suddenly, Jerry got an idea to distract the cat. He bought a cup of milk and a fish and kept it under its mouth. When it was drinking the milk, Jenny escaped. They both ran towards their group. Their parents were so happy to have them back.

Moral of the story: Never leave a friend behind and they will not leave you.

STRANGE DISAPPEARANCES
Sunanditha Shree 8C

Chapter-1

March 20, 2100,

Technology is crazy and cool at this point of time, and nothing can be done without the help of robots. Many of the crazy inventions are the Time Machine, the Multiplier, and Smart Pet, to name a few.

Well, I am sure everyone knows what a time machine is, so, I will move on to the Multiplier, which is basically a machine which can copy objects. The Smart Pet is a robot available in many types such as the dog, the cat, the fish, and every possible animal. It can speak in any language and be your assistant, tell facts, crack jokes, and uplift your mood like a human being.

The world did have these technologies, but people never cared about nature, plants, and animals. Since they had The Multiplier, no one had to take the care of growing crops. Same goes for animal-obtained food. People had the Smart Pet and so no one really wanted a dog, a cat, or any other animal as a pet.

People slowly started to turn their faces away from zoos, natural parks, and wildlife sanctuaries. The forests which remained were chopped down, the wood was useless and was burnt, the land was used to build stuff, and the animals were simply shot down in the name of "Shooting Championships".

Also, Global Warming was high, and people lived in heat-proof capsule-like houses. Children attended online classes, and people didn't go out for anything unnecessary. Even if they did, they wore heat-proof suits. Even in their capsule-like homes, no one talked a lot. Most of the day, everyone's eyes were glued to cell phones and other devices.

In this crisis, only one forest remained in the world. It was big and had many types of trees and animals. Those were the last surviving species other than humans. Do you know who protected this forest? Let's find out.

A few meters away from this forest, there lived the Pinewood family. The family had Mr. William Pinewood, Mrs. Laurine Pinewood, July Pinewood, Anthony Pinewood, the 10-year-old and the youngest in the family, and Chip, a 'real' dog, a Siberian Husky, to be specific. They were a happy family. But how do they protect the forest?

The entire forest, all that land is written in the family's name. It's their plot of land, so no one can do anything to it. Mr. Pinewood is a Botanist, he studies plants while Mrs. Pinewood is a Zoologist, she studies animals, and July is an inventor, she invents technology to sustain the forest and protect it from the unbearable heat. They are not a normal family; they are a type of family whom we can see in 2022. Talking, playing, and eating together, they do all of this while not saying no to technology. They too have technology just like a modern family.

One day, while Mr. Pinewood and Mrs. Pinewood were looking around the forest, Mr. Pinewood spotted a pit in the middle of the forest. He recognized the spot, it was where Mahogany 54-C would stand, or used to stand. The pit happened to be the entire plant uprooted from the spot, no human could do that, and no person or robot could sneak into the forest. It was of no use for them anyway.

"Mahogany 54-C is missing!" he said. Mrs. Pinewood looked shocked too. "Baloo and her cub always stay in this cave during this time. They are missing too!".

Strange disappearances of animals and trees continued in the forest. Everyone was scared and confused. July checked the security system twice, yet it showed no sign of trespassing. But the trees were not cut, they were uprooted. It was strange.

Anthony wasn't going to let the "forest thief", as he called it, get away with this.

Chapter-2
Catching the Forest Thief

So, one dark night, he quietly snuck out of bed and went into the forest. As he walked through the forest, he heard chirping crickets, howling wolves, hooting owls and the wind singing a song equally scary. Anthony was scared.

Suddenly, he heard sounds of walking on the crisp leaves. Anthony ran and stood still after a while. He saw a blurry figure, with some streaks of green, illuminating.

Anthony was scared and awestruck. He couldn't see the figure properly, except for the green lights. As he watched on, a wolf ran towards the figure, but the figure to a strange gun, shot the wolf, and a blue beam of light came out of it. The wolf's howling ceased.

Anthony could see that the wolf was frozen in its place and didn't move. Suddenly, the figure pressed a button on a remote-like machine, and "POOF"! The figure and the wolf disappeared!

Anthony was overwhelmed with fright, and he ran towards his house. He just tucked in his bed and encased himself in his blanket, followed by fitful nightmares disturbing his sleep.

Next day, everyone sat at the dining table, where Anthony told the entire incident. Mr. & Mrs. Pinewood laughed out loud, and Mr. Pinewood only replied, "Son, I told you to not eat those extra chocolates in the fridge. Do you know, eating at night, right before you sleep can cause nightmares?"

Mrs. Pinewood then said, "Anthony, listen, it's all a dream. No one has teleportation and freezing guns in this time. I am sure if this is real, it can only be an alien, or a dream. Honey, this is not an alien, this is just a vivid imagination."

But July was struck when she heard the word alien. She thought

Anthony might have told the truth. So, after breakfast, she called Anthony. "Listen brother, I have full trust in you, and I believe you aren't lying. So, I have decided that we both go into the woods tomorrow. Stay awake."

That night, July and Anthony walked into the woods. It seemed they came early that night, so, they were searching around the lake. July had a camera in her hands and was ready to take any photos or videos with it.

Suddenly, they heard a sound from inside the lake, and July started shooting the video. Meanwhile, something rose out of the lake, it was a spaceship, and from that spaceship appeared an alien! It had a thin green body; a head shaped like an upside-down egg, almond-shaped eyes, and had a remote-like machine and a strange gun in its hands.

The alien walked down the spaceship. Just then, it pressed a button on the remote, and the spaceship sank under the water of lake. The alien then saw a herd of female deer and their fawns, sleeping on the ground. The alien shot the does and the fawns, one by one. Then, pressing the button, it disappeared along with the deer.

July had already shot a video the whole scene. Anthony and July ran back home and snuck into bed.

The next day, Anthony and July told their parents everything and showed the video. Mr. and Mrs. Pinewood could not believe that an alien had come to the forest. They discussed a plan to catch hold of the alien. A plan had finally struck Anthony and he told it to everyone.

After some days of discussions and deliberations, one night, the plan was executed. The alien had just started to do what it always did, when it suddenly saw Chip barking at it and sitting beside a boulder covered with vines.

The alien then said, "%^$&@! @&^#%^@'\;±§*." (English Translation: "A new animal! I must catch it before it runs away.) The alien talked in a language called §&^%, (English Translation: Keplish).

Then, the alien took out its gun when Chip started to bite the vines. The vines were cut, and the alien was trapped in a cage which dropped from above. The Pinewoods came out of their hiding spots and everyone cheered and hugged Chip! He had caught the Forest Thief!

What intentions did the alien have? Were they good or bad? Let's find out.

Chapter-3
Interrogating the Thief

It was March 25, the next day after capturing the alien. Anthony thought of handing the alien over to the police. But Mr. Pinewood didn't agree. He said, "Anthony, I am sure the police will send the alien to the lab for experiments and will kill it. It is better we find out why it is doing this." Anthony was convinced.

Mrs. Pinewood was in deep thought. She remembered that about 7 years ago, her old friend Susan, who was an astronaut, had claimed that she had seen aliens during one of her inter-stellar missions to Kepler 452B, one of the earth-like planets. She also claimed that she had stayed with aliens for 5 years, learned their ways and language, and the aliens rebuilt her spacecraft which had crashed on the surface.

So that night, she had called Susan, who was more than delighted to speak to an old friend after a long time. Mrs. Pinewood said, "Susan, it's nice to talk after a long time. How are you?" Susan replied, "Laurine, it's been a long time, I am fine. How are you?" "I am fine too. I've called you for a very important matter."

Mrs. Pinewood explained everything, and Susan took the car to Mrs. Pinewood's house. Mrs. Pinewood took her to the room where the alien was kept. Susan locked the door and after 5 hours, she came out. Susan started to tell everything to the family.

"The alien is from Kepler 452B. It was very curious about Earth after I left. They call Earth the Goolia. Anyway, he sent a boxbot, which is like the satellite we send to other planets."

Suddenly, Mr. Pinewood interrupted and asked, "Then we could have found the boxbot before itself." Susan felt a bit irritated but continued, "The boxbot is so small that even a fly cannot see it. Unlike satellites, these can go near to the planet's surface and see everything." The alien researched using the boxbot for 7 years, until it found out that humans were destroying nature and its creatures, and they only cared about themselves. It also discovered the last forest on earth, which is on your plot of land. So, it decided to save nature and its creatures and came to Earth. It came to Earth and would freeze animals and plants in time, take them to its spaceship, and preserve it until it went back to Kepler 452B."

"I have told it that you are all good humans who only think for the good of the forest. So, the alien has kept a condition, that if humans don't change in 3 months, he would take all the animals and plants in the forest and would give humans 6 months' time. If they didn't change, he would bring the alien army and destroy humanity and would rule the planet like how it was supposed to be, living with nature without harming it."

Well, will humanity change? Will the aliens destroy us? Let's find out.

Chapter-4
The End (Of What?)

It was early morning on December 25, 2100, Christmas. This date was the one which would define the fate of humanity. This year, it was the day which was nine months after the day Susan interrogated the alien. Meanwhile, the alien had been released and it had gone back to Kepler 452B.

Coming back, Anthony, July and Chip were playing on the field. Yes, you heard me right, I did say field. The alien, according to his promise, had taken away the entire forest. Now, the only species on earth; other than humans, were the plants in the Pinewoods' house, and Chip.

Coming back, as they were playing, Anthony gazed into the sky, to see the sun being covered by a black shadow. "A Solar Eclipse?" thought July. She knew what to do. Looking down at the grass, she closed Anthony's eyes and pulled him into the house, where she closed the windows and the curtains.

But soon, the light come out through a hole on one of the curtains. A curious Chip opened the window to see the sun was shining. There were many spaceships landing on the ground. From them, emerged thousands and thousands of aliens, with high tech weapons. One of them shot a laser beam from its gun towards Anthony and –

"Anthony! Wake up! You made a promise that you'll wake up early during the spring vacations! Get up sleepy head! July's already up and eating breakfast! GET UP!"

Anthony raised his sleepy head out of the blanket. He was scared and was shivering with fright. Seeing this, Mrs. Pinewood said, "What happened Anthony? You're shivering. Do you have a fever?" Anthony didn't reply, instead he said, "PAT (Personal Amigo Tech), what is the date today?" He had talked to a toy dog, which was a voice assistant. It replied, "The date today is 26 March 2100.

Mrs. Pinewood was confused. She asked, "Tell me, what happened, did you have a dream?" Anthony just replied, "Oh yes, I had a dream, and a very, very terrible one." Anthony told everything and Mrs. Pinewood just said, "It's fine, it's just a dream. Get up and brush your teeth, I've made porridge for breakfast."

Anthony told his dream to Mr. Pinewood and July at the table. July said, "My, that's a terrible dream indeed. If we don't do anything, this Christmas will be the last and worst one ever."

About the alien, it was a complete weirdo, and it ate very weird food. Sometimes, it ate a few weird plants, colored in violet, or would fry them in some gooey liquid, which was stickier than oil. Also, the liquid could only cook if kept in low temperatures.

Ironically, it thought our food grains, vegetables and fruits were weirder, especially cauliflowers, kidney beans and strawberries. But it was a kind soul. It never ate other animals, unlike us.

Mr. and Mrs. Pinewood, along with Susan decided to reveal the alien to the public. So, they did. The alien was quite happy. He made speeches, suggestions and advice for the people, but none could quite understand. So, Susan used to stand and translate the whatever the alien said.

But some people thought the alien was a very skinny, weird-faced human, painted in green. They also thought that the alien and the others had ganged up to make lies and stop technology growth.

To prove that it was not a human, or as it called us #$:{]^ (English: Goolian), it took a DNA Test, which showed that it had absolutely no similarity between humans, that is 0%. Since the test result was zero, the rumors were proved untrue.

The alien also wanted to learn English. Just then, it went into July's room, to see all the English AuDictionaries, stacked on a cupboard shelf. "#@\\Y @}{||^\\! @&#^@* @&, (&@{](@&. _(@&! &@^@%@! (An English AuDictionary! Wait, I have the Keplish AuDictionary. So, I can learn English using them!)

So, it took the Keplish AuDictionary, compared them with the English AuDictionary and learned English in just 5 hours! An audbook is a flat card with a play button on it. If it is clicked, it plays the entire book as an audio.

When the alien saw Anthony come, it talked in English, "Hey little Goolian! Seems that you are surprised." Anthony froze in his place. "What! How… How c… could…you… t…ta…talk…in English!

The alien explained everything and called Mr. & Mrs. Pinewood and July. They were as surprised as Anthony. He talked in English during speeches and more than everyone, Susan was more relieved. Her mouth had started hurting because of the continuous hours of talking. The alien's speech was at least 5 hours long!

Soon, the alien had to travel back to Kepler 452B. It went and the Pinewoods tried their best to make humanity change. Some did but most of them didn't change. Since the day the alien left, each day passed like a bolt of lightning. But very few people changed.

3 Months passed and, according to the alien's promise, it came, when the clock struck 12. It took away the entire forest, as if it were covered with an invisibility cloak. It was a huge shock for the Pinewoods and the world. The alien's promise had come true. Fear spread over the world.

No one could believe what had happened. Like Anthony's dream, Now, the only species on earth; other than humans, were the plants in the Pinewoods' house and Chip. It was something the world couldn't imagine.

Fear had struck the hearts of the humans. They wanted to mend their ways. As they were doing so, the alien who watched everything through the boxbot, was pleased. It immediately came to earth with many spaceships. But it didn't come to destroy humanity.

The alien and its kind revealed a huge secret. They had been collecting plants and animals since generations! Everyone was happy as they could bring more extinct animals and plants back to life. Soon, the trees and plants were unfrozen by the aliens and were planted in old cities, in this time, cities become old in less than one month. The animals and birds were unfrozen and let in after the forests were complete. The aliens shared many inventions that helped to survive with nature.

Humanity moved towards renewable energy and governments were given funds by the people themselves. The aliens used the Carbon-Dioxide Remover, which took Carbon-Dioxide out of the atmosphere, and helped humans to use the Carbon-Dioxide as fuel without emissions.

Christmas came and the Earth was beautiful. For the first time, people could come out of the house without heat-proof suits. Everyone celebrated the real Christmas, spending time with each other. Christmas before was just to buy a Decorated-Christmas Tree, take a photo and put it on social media. Everyone had not only saved the Earth, but they also learned the value of spending time together.

Many years (And many Christmases) later…

The day is December 25, 2120, Christmas. Mr. & Mrs. Pinewood were old, and Anthony was all grown up. Both the siblings were married and were living a happy life with their family. Mr. & Mrs. Pinewood were telling the exact story I told you all to their grandchildren.

"But, Grandma, what happened to the aliens?" asked June, July's eldest daughter. "Ah, they went back to Kepler 452B after New Year. They were such caring creatures. We have a lot to learn from them." said Mrs. Pinewood, in a quiet sad tone.

"Will they ever come back, Grandpa." Asked Kevin, Anthony's

youngest son. "Well, the aliens will not come back. But if we start harming Mother Earth again, they will come and destroy us." Replied Mr. Pinewood.

"Okay kids don't ask too many questions. The Pie is ready. Thanks, brother, for helping me with it." Said July.

Just then, from inside the kitchen appeared Anthony. "My pleasure, Sister. We did need to bake a lot as we have some special guests coming." Mr. & Mrs. Pinewood thought it must have been their new neighbors, the Browns.

Just then, the doorbell rang. "They must be here", thought Mr. & Mrs. Pinewood as they walked towards the door. When they opened it, they heard a weird voice say, "Merry Christmas from Kepler 452B!" Guess what, there were the aliens! Anthony and July had transmitted some signals through space to call the aliens home for Christmas!

The children were most surprised to see the aliens. They talked with them, ate pie with them and played with them all day. That was how ended a Christmas with aliens.

HOPE
Swetha Krishna 11 A

In a world once pure, nature used to sing,
now it wails, burdened by climate's cruel sting.
A fragile balance disrupted, harmony undone,
as our planet weeps, wounded by the warming sun.
Glaciers cry as their tears flow into the river,
as greed-fuelled flames continue to quiver.
Their icy beauty melts into the sea,
drowning the hopes of a future yet to be.
Oceans suffer, choked by plastic's blight,
their vibrant depths fading from our sight.
Creatures struggle, their homes polluted,
as nature weeps at the pain of being looted.
Yet hope persists among our youth,
as humans rise to bring light to the truth.
Together we plant seeds of change,
embracing a future where heat doesn't pain.
We control emissions, do what's right,
unite as caretakers, in nature's sacred fight.
Let's mend the wounds, one by one
and pass it on to those to come.

THERE IS ENOUGH FOR EVERYONE'S NEEDS BUT NOT FOR THEIR GREED
Vaibhavi Verma 11A

In this modern existence,
From early infancy,
we have all been taught how to lead.
We have been trained to just succeed.
due to which the limits of the rules of life
we exceed We learn, we read,
and when we get a vocation, we proceed.
Life flashes with speed.
but in this journey, we're never freed.
Though this is indeed what we need.
But there is the most dangerous human trait, called greed.
This avidity leads people to steal.
With no reason, there is this desire,
increasing like a forest fire,
The more we try to calm it down,
the more it increases.
Though it is not required, we all still acquire.
Today's individuals want success.
with no pain, and no bleed.

65

If they get a chance to win, they might even plead.
Everyone seems to believe,
They will get it without hard work or good deeds.
In this modern existence,
There is enough for everyone's needs.
but not for their greed.

APPEARANCE IS NOT EVERYTHING

Yazhini Kannan Yadav 6E

This story is about a girl named Angela Isabella who was eleven years old. She was living in Canada with her parents. She had beautiful smooth blonde hair with a beautiful and attractive face which shone as bright as gold. She had been studying in her school ever since kindergarten. She was good at studies and had a lot of friends. So now, let's get into the story.

One fine day, while she was walking down the school corridors with her friends, she spotted a little girl who looked younger than her getting bullied. She did not bother and left minding her own business. That night she could not sleep because she felt bad for the little girl.

The next day, when she reached the school, she noticed that her best friend Luna was bullying the little girl. She ran to the little girl and told her friend "My friend, why are you bullying this little girl over here?" After seeing her, her friend felt ashamed and ran away.

Then she went near the little girl, and saw that she had very messy and tangled hair and she was very fat. She asked her why everyone had been bullying her. The little girl said that "Everyone is bullying me for my appearance, I wish I could be beautiful like you."

These words touched her heart. She felt deeply saddened because everyone in her school seemed to judge each other based on their outward appearances rather than their inner qualities. She imagined the countless children who might have been subjected to bullying because of their looks. She knew she had to put a full stop to this problem.

The next day she got permission to meet their Principal Ms. Anna, who was very kind and caring towards students. She explained to her about the problems faced by the children who are getting bullied. She also explained how other children were looking at each other's appearance instead of their behavior or character. Then the principal decided to make a new rule called ANTI-BULLYING. The rule was that, people who bullies others will get punished. The next day she noticed that nobody was bullying each other. The whole day there was a big smile in her face.

LIFE AIN'T A GAME
Nehrin Riyaz 4 E

Life ain't a game,
It's a battle for fame. Find your name, Don't be so lame.
Life ain't nice, You need to rise. Shake the dice,
You always won't get something nice.
Now choose your will, And earn that fame.
Take a leap, have faith,
Don't be shy, for you are game.

SOMEONE LIKE YOU

Time changes, but not you. Especially someone like you.
Someone glowing like a star,
The power of gamma rays from far.
There are only a few, And a teacher like you.
Without you, I'd be nowhere. You and a few made me shine,
 Like a sun everywhere.
Previously, I reflected (like a moon),
But you made me shine, my own light. I was a chunk of metal,
But you and a few forged me. And it was done gracefully.

(dedicated to all the teachers in my life)

www.ingramcontent.com/pod-product-compliance
Lightning Source LLC
LaVergne TN
LVHW041751190726
843493LV00008B/2556